SECRETS

OF THE

ANIMAL WORLD

CAMELS
Ships of the Desert

by Eulalia García
Illustrated by Gabriel Casadevall and Ali Garousi

Gareth Stevens Publishing
MILWAUKEE

For a free color catalog describing Gareth Stevens' list of high-quality books, call 1-800-542-2595 (USA) or 1-800-461-9120 (Canada). Gareth Stevens' Fax: (414) 225-0377.

The editor would like to extend special thanks to Richard Sajdak, Aquarium and Reptile Curator, Milwaukee County Zoo, Milwaukee, Wisconsin, for his kind and professional help with the information in this book.

Library of Congress Cataloging-in-Publication Data

García, Eulalia.
   [Camello. English]
   Camels: ships of the desert / by Eulalia García; illustrated by Gabriel Casadevall and Ali Garousi.
     p. cm. — (Secrets of the animal world)
   Includes bibliographical references (p.) and index.
   Summary: Provides detailed information on the physical characteristics and behavior of camels.
   ISBN 0-8368-1494-0 (lib. bdg.)
   1. Camels—Juvenile literature. [1. Camels.] I. Casadevall, Gabriel, ill. II. Garousi, Ali, ill. III. Title. IV. Series.
QL737.U54G3613 1996
599.73'6—dc20   95-45835

This North American edition first published in 1996 by
Gareth Stevens Publishing
1555 North RiverCenter Drive, Suite 201
Milwaukee, Wisconsin 53212 USA

This U.S. edition © 1996 by Gareth Stevens, Inc. Created with original © 1993 Ediciones Este, S.A., Barcelona, Spain. Additional end matter © 1996 by Gareth Stevens, Inc.

Series editor: Patricia Lantier-Sampon
Editorial assistants: Diane Laska, Jamie Daniel, Rita Reitci

Printed in the United States of America

1 2 3 4 5 6 7 8 9 99 98 97 96

CONTENTS

THE WORLD OF THE CAMEL

Where do camels live?

Most people think camels live only in deserts, but not all of them do. The two camel species are: African, or dromedaries, which have a single hump; and Bactrians, which have two. Dromedaries are domesticated animals that travel in Tuareg and Bedouin caravans. They live in northern Africa and the Near East. Bactrian camels take their name from the kingdom of Bactria, which no longer exists, and live in Central Asia, Iran, the Gobi Desert, and even in the Himalayas at altitudes of up to 13,000 feet (4,000 meters).

The Bactrian camel's thick coat provides protection against the cold.

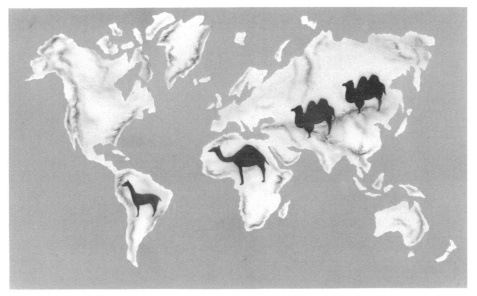

Camels live in northern Africa, the Near East, Central Asia, Mongolia, and the Himalayas. Other members of the camel family live in the Andean Cordillera in South America.

Desert life

Living in a desert environment is difficult, but many animals thrive despite the lack of water and extreme temperatures. Daytime temperatures of 140°F (60°C) can suddenly drop to below 32°F (0°C) at night. Camels can go for more than fifteen days without drinking while carrying a heavy load across large stretches of desert. They save, or conserve, water by not sweating, urinating very little, and making the most of the sparse desert food.

Lack of water is the main problem for desert animals.

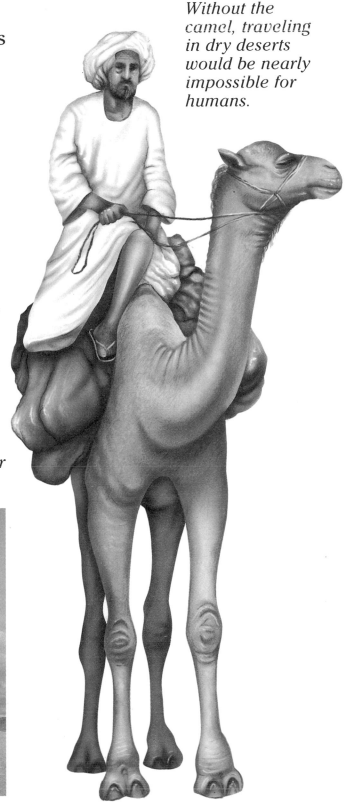

Without the camel, traveling in dry deserts would be nearly impossible for humans.

Camels and their relatives

Camels are ruminants that belong to the scientific family Camelidae. A common feature is their ability to adapt to harsh environments, such as deserts, steppes, and high altitudes. Dromedaries and Bactrian camels are easily recognizable by their humps. Bactrian camels are sturdier than

Members of the camel family.

VICUÑA

LLAMA

GUANACO

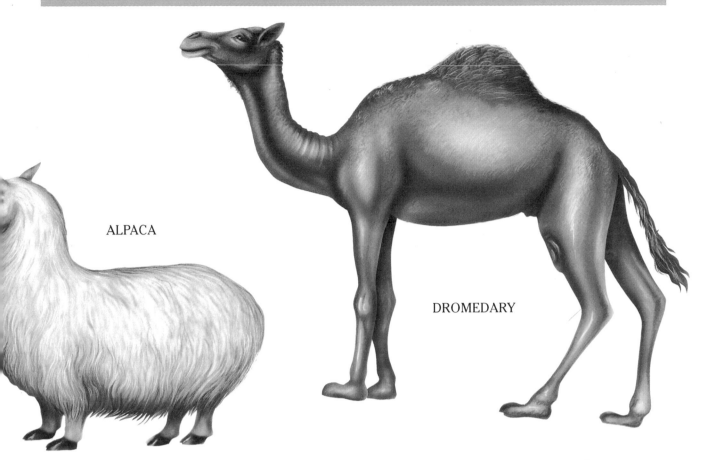

ALPACA

DROMEDARY

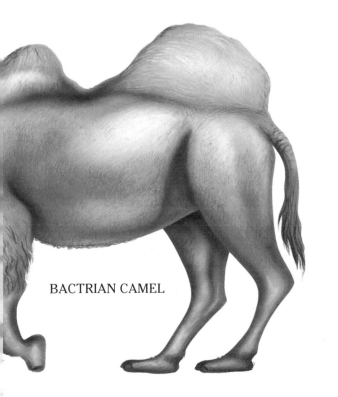

BACTRIAN CAMEL

dromedaries and have shorter legs and a longer, thicker coat around their head and neck. Ruminants from South America include llamas and vicuñas, as well as guanacos and alpacas.

The camel family is valuable to humans because the animals provide meat, skins, and milk. They are also useful as beasts of burden for carrying heavy loads as well as humans on long journeys across deserts or through mountains.

INSIDE THE CAMEL

CRANIAL SINUS
Empty space in the bones of the nose. When the camel inhales, the sinus humidifies incoming air. When it exhales, the sinus collects water from the air leaving the lungs.

EYES
Long eyelashes protect eyes from sun and sand.

NAPE GLAND
Gland at the nape of the neck that releases an attractive smell for other camels during mating season. When courtship begins, the camels rub and twist their necks together.

NASAL PASSAGES
The camel can close its nostrils completely to protect nasal passages from the sand.

HARD PALATE

TEETH

LIPS
Upper lip is split into two parts to reach food more easily. Lower lip has a thick, hard edge for picking spiny vegetation.

SOFT PALATE

TRACHEA

ESOPHAGUS

NECK

HEART

SALIVARY GLANDS
Help the camel digest vegetables by first breaking them down in its mouth.

The largest of all desert mammals, the dromedary is referred to as "king of the desert" because it has adapted itself so perfectly to this harsh environment. The camel has changed its shape and behavior over millions of years. For example, it hardly sweats, which is a good way to save water. Its feet are also padded for walking on the sand.

SOLE OF FOOT
On each foot, the camel has a padded sole with two toes that spread wide. This distributes the camel's weight over a large area so it will not sink in the sand.

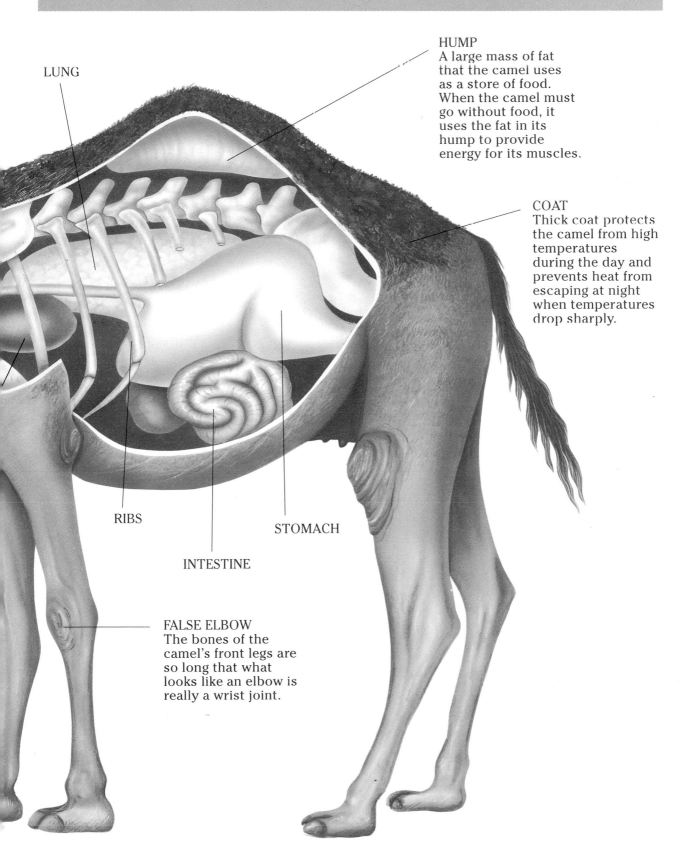

LUNG

HUMP
A large mass of fat
that the camel uses
as a store of food.
When the camel must
go without food, it
uses the fat in its
hump to provide
energy for its muscles.

COAT
Thick coat protects
the camel from high
temperatures
during the day and
prevents heat from
escaping at night
when temperatures
drop sharply.

RIBS

STOMACH

INTESTINE

FALSE ELBOW
The bones of the
camel's front legs are
so long that what
looks like an elbow is
really a wrist joint.

SHIP OF THE DESERT

Camels and temperature

Desert dwellers put their camels to work when the animals are still very young. At first, the camels walk only about 18 miles (30 kilometers) a day, carrying loads of about 330 pounds (150 kilograms). But they also struggle against lack of water and burning heat. Because there is so little water, the camels save as much as possible. They allow their body temperature to rise

After a long trek, both camels and their riders need a rest.

INTERMEDIATE POSITION
A camel may some-times place itself slightly turned toward the sun.

UNFAVORABLE POSITION
Standing sideways, the camel receives the sun's rays directly and can become too warm.

IDEAL POSITION
The camel turns its back to the sun to avoid its rays.

INTERMEDIATE POSITION

UNFAVORABLE POSITION

as high as 106°F (41°C). This reduces the difference between the outside temperature and the body temperature, which then reduces the need to sweat in order to cool down. Their thick summer coat also works as insulation to keep the camels from becoming too warm.

A thick coat protects the dromedary from desert heat and the Bactrian from the cold.

IDEAL POSITION

that camels can be stubborn and lazy?

Although camels appear calm and docile, they change moods easily. When loads are too heavy, the animals get angry and bellow in protest. During mating season, males are sometimes bad-tempered and refuse to carry riders or loads. When South American llamas are tired or too heavily burdened, they lie down and simply refuse to get up. The only solution is to lighten the load; no other method will work.

Kings of the desert

For thousands of years, camels have enabled humans to travel through the desert. Horses, mules, and donkeys cannot remain standing for long without sinking into the fine sand. A camel's feet, however, have pads that prevent the animal from sinking. Its eyes are covered by long, woven eyelashes that protect them from sandstorms and the strong sunshine. The camel can also close its nostrils to prevent sand from entering.

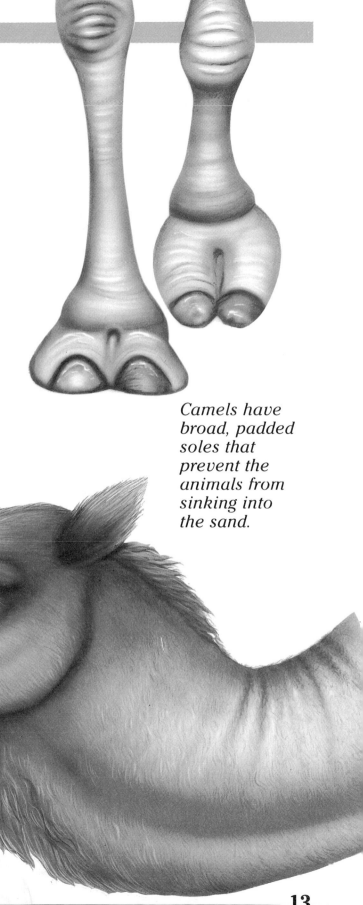

Camels have broad, padded soles that prevent the animals from sinking into the sand.

Camels have thick eyelashes that help protect their eyes.

13

FALSE WATER TANK

Getting by on very little

It was a popular belief until recently that camels kept water in their hump, but this is not true. The fat of the hump acts as insulation against the heat and as a store of food. A camel's hump can show the animal's state of health. An upright hump indicates that the camel

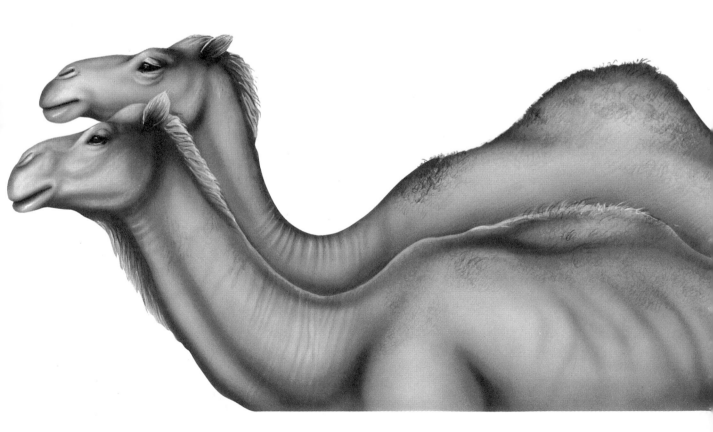

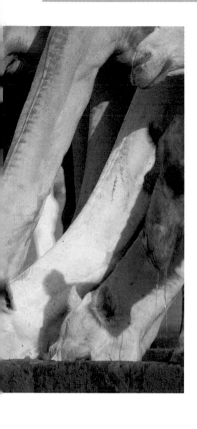

Camels can go without drinking any water for weeks, but at times they drink huge amounts of water.

has had plenty of food and rest. A shrunken hump shows that the camel is tired, sick, or has not eaten for a long time.

When the camel cannot find water, it uses water stored in its body tissues. A camel can lose up to 25 percent of its weight in water and still remain active. To replace this water, a camel can drink 33 gallons (125 liters) in ten minutes.

The camel's hump contains a store of fat that can be burned up as food for energy.

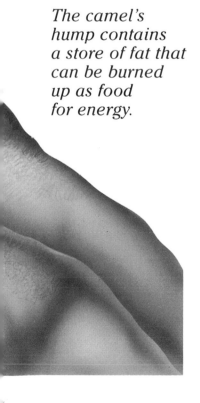

Camels also obtain water from vegetation they eat.

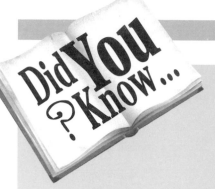

that camels wear kneepads?

Camels have patches of hard skin on their knees, wrists, and the lower part of the trunk that act as kneepads. These rough areas help support the camel's body weight when it is in a sitting position. A camel's legs are very long in comparison to the rest of its body, but these long legs help keep its trunk from the hot sands. The camel's small head is 10 feet (3 meters) from the ground when it stretches its neck. This allows the camel to reach small blades of grass on the ground.

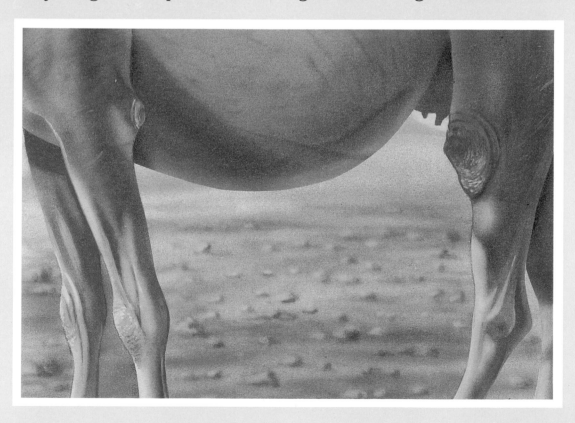

Finding food in the desert

Camels can eat thorny desert plants. To help digest these plants, camels have a complex stomach with three chambers that store food for a long time. The camel grips a plant with its thick, hard lips and cuts it into small pieces that go into the first chamber. After a few hours, the remains of this food return to the mouth, where they are chewed and mixed with saliva. The food then moves into the second chamber and from there into the third to complete the digestive process.

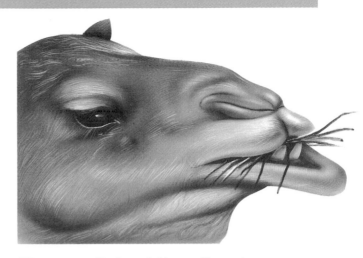

The camel's hard lips allow it to pluck tough, thorny desert plants.

Lack of water in a desert means that only a few plants exist. Camels, however, know how to make the most of them.

THE CAMEL'S ANCESTORS

The first camels

Camels first appeared 40 million years ago, mainly in North America. At first they were similar to rabbits, with four toes on each foot and shorter forelegs than hind legs. One early camel was Protylopus, only 20 inches (50 cm) long. The Poebrotherium of North America looked more like a present-day camel. Heavier camels also evolved in North

Despite its resemblance to a giraffe, the Alticamelus also had camel-like features.

America, such as Alticamelus, a long-necked, giraffelike camel, and the Titanotylopus, up to 11.5 feet (3.5 meters) tall.

Poebrotherium was a small animal about the size of a sheep that resembled the modern camel. It lived in North America, along with certain species of primitive elephants, horses, and rhinoceroses of the time.

Primitive Protylopus was about the size of a rabbit.

Camels spread throughout North America, from Florida to Alaska, and also to Asia across the Bering Strait. For reasons that remain unknown, camels disappeared from North America about ten thousand years ago, but they have continued their evolution in South America, Asia, and Africa.

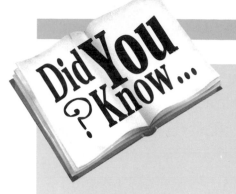

Did **You** ? **Know** ...

that some camels pull sleds?

Camels have always been dependable in spite of their unpredictable character. They are the animals best suited to life in the desert. Bactrian camels, however, can also work in the cold and snow. These two-humped camels are hardier than their African relatives. Bactrians are also quieter, more obedient, and more affectionate with their owners. Bactrians pull sleds loaded with goods in the snowy areas of Asia.

HOW CAMELS LIVE

Camels and humans

Camels and humans have lived together for a long, long time. The camel is more useful for desert dwellers than the seal is for the Inuit or the bison once was for the American Indians. Besides providing food, camels can carry riders and loads, pull plows, and turn the sails of a mill. Camel hair is used to make blankets, fabric, and rope. Humans use two types of camels: riding camels and carrier camels. Riding camels

Camel caravans allow desert dwellers to trade supplies and other goods.

are large with a slender trunk, thin legs, and small head. Carrier camels are sturdier, with a thicker trunk, larger head, and smaller overall size.

In certain areas of the world, camels replace horses and oxen in farming.

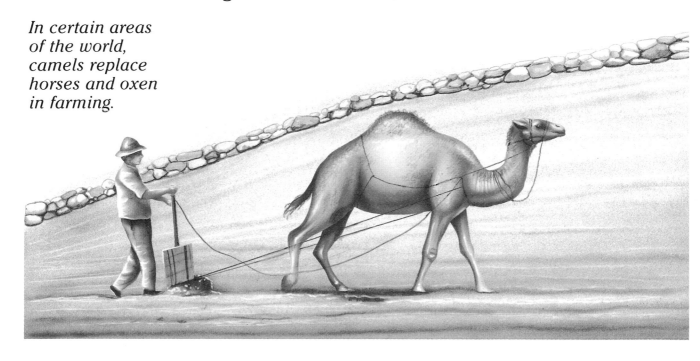

South American relatives

Camels are perhaps the ideal means of transportation in sandy or snowy areas. But llamas, vicuñas, guanacos, and alpacas have adapted themselves to the bare rocks of the Andean cordillera at altitudes of 13,125 to 16,400 feet (4,000 to 5,000 m). These domesticated animals are used for meat, wool, and as beasts of burden. Vicuñas live in herds consisting

South American vicuñas walk nimbly over the steep, rocky mountainsides of the Andes.

During mating season, male guanacos kick and bite each other in fierce competition.

In a herd, the male protects the females from predators such as the puma.

of several females and a single male that constantly keeps watch. When he sees a possible sign of danger, he whistles to warn the females. He is the last to run as they escape. Guanacos also live in herds led by a dominant male. During mating season, the male follows the female closely so that another male will not intrude. When this does happen, however, the two males fight, striking each other with their front feet until the matter is settled. The female gives birth usually to one baby guanaco after a six-month gestation period.

APPENDIX TO

SECRETS OF THE ANIMAL WORLD

CAMELS
Ships of the Desert

CAMEL SECRETS

More stubborn than a camel.
When their camels refuse to
move, the Tuaregs frighten the
animals with a flaming torch.

▼ The wool of the alpaca suri.
The valuable coat of this camel
relative has fibers as long as
20 inches (50 cm).

Are camels brave? During
their travels, camels may
sometimes stop suddenly and
refuse to continue when they
see an unknown object on the
ground, even though it may
be harmless.

▼ Guanaco habits. Guanacos like
to roll in mud and always do so in
the same place until they have dug
a hole in the ground. They also
leave their excrement in the same
place until it forms a pile.

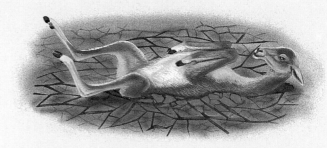

Exported camels. Dromedaries
and Bactrian camels can be found
in places far from their points of
origin. Some even live in Australia
and the Canary Islands.

Pacing. This step is unusual among mammals in the wild. It consists of moving both legs on the same side together in the same direction. Pacing seems to be a fast way of crossing open spaces.

▶ **The Bactrian camel's coat.** When summer heat arrives, Bactrian camels lose their coats in tufts, giving them a sad, moth-eaten appearance.

1. What do camels do to prevent sweating?
a) Avoid moving.
b) Increase body temperature.
c) Lower body temperature.

2. Camels save water by:
a) urinating frequently.
b) sweating frequently.
c) sweating and urinating only very little.

3. The camel's coat:
a) gives it a better appearance.
b) has no real value.
c) protects it from cold and heat.

4. Where and how does the camel store its water?
a) In the fat of the pads of its feet.
b) In the tissues of its body.
c) In its three stomach chambers.

5. Llamas, vicuñas, guanacos, and alpacas are camel relatives in:
a) England.
b) South America.
c) Alaska.

6. What is a camel's stomach like?
a) It is divided into three chambers.
b) It is a single, large chamber.
c) It is divided into four chambers.

The answers to CAMEL SECRETS questions are on page 32.

GLOSSARY

adaptation: the way a living organism changes its behaviors and needs in order to survive in different conditions.

ancestors: previous generations; predecessors.

Bactrian camels: camels with two humps, named after the ancient country of Bactria in western Asia.

Bedouins: Arab people of Asia and North Africa who traditionally wander from place to place, live in tents, and raise herds of animals that travel with them.

burden: a heavy load.

caravan: a group of people who travel together, usually with vehicles or pack animals.

conserve: to use something carefully in such a way that it isn't hurt or used up.

cordillera: a chain of mountains.

deserts: extremely dry areas, often covered in sand, in which there is very little water. Deserts are usually very hot during the day but cooler at night.

digestive process: the way our systems break down what we eat so that our bodies can receive necessary nutrients. An animal's digestive process depends on the food available in its environment.

docile: mild-tempered and good-natured.

domesticated: tamed; trained.

dominant: having the most authority or control.

dromedaries: camels with one hump. Dromedaries are native to Arabia and Africa.

environment: the surroundings in which plants, animals, and other organisms live. Most camels live in a hot desert environment, but some can also thrive in a cold mountainous environment.

evolution: to change shape or develop gradually over a long period of time.

excrement: the solid waste matter that leaves an animal's body after it has processed its food. Excrement contains matter the animal's body cannot use.

gestation period: the time period in the reproductive cycle from conception to the birth of an animal.

glands: organs in the body that make and release substances such as sweat, tears, and saliva.

guanaco: a South American ruminant believed to be the ancestor of the llama and alpaca, which have been domesticated.

hardy: strong and healthy.

Himalayas: a mountain range about 1,500 miles (2,400 km) long that runs between India and Tibet.

humidify: to add moisture to the air.

insulation: a layer of a substance or material that offers protection against extreme cold and heat.

intermediate: a position that is located between or in the middle of something.

mammals: warm-blooded animals that have backbones. Female mammals produce milk to feed their young.

modify: to change something, usually in an attempt to improve it.

nape: the back of the neck.

nasal passages: hollow passages in the head that allow air to pass through the nose and head into the lungs.

nimbly: quickly and easily.

palate: the roof of the mouth, which is usually made up of two parts: a bony front part, called the hard palate; and a soft back part that can move, called the soft palate.

primitive: of or relating to an early and usually simple stage of development.

ruminants: even-toed animals that chew cuds and that have three or four stomach chambers for digesting their food. Camels, giraffes, cows, deer, and sheep are ruminants.

saliva: the fluid made by glands in the mouth to keep the mouth moist and to help in chewing, swallowing, and digesting food.

sole: the bottom surface of the foot or hoof.

sparse: thin and scattered.

species: animals or plants that are closely related and often similar in behavior and appearance. Members of the same species are capable of breeding together.

steppe: a vast, level, plain — usually without trees.

terrain: the physical features of a piece of land.

thrive: to develop and maintain a healthy condition.

trek: a trip or journey.

trunk: the main part of the body.

Tuaregs: traditional, nomadic people of the Sahara Desert.

ACTIVITIES

◆ Visit the nearest zoo and look at the camels. Does the zoo house both Bactrians and dromedaries? Do any of the camel's relatives, such as llamas or alpacas, also live at the zoo? How are these animals alike, and how are they different?

◆ Go to the library and find a book on the deserts that camels inhabit in Africa and the Middle East. Find out what other animals inhabit these deserts. Compare what you discover with the animals that inhabit a typical desert in the American Southwest.

◆ Go to the library and find out which areas of the world use camels as work animals. Why are camels better for the work they do than horses or donkeys? What characteristics make them better for working in certain environments?

MORE BOOKS TO READ

All about Deserts. John Sanders (Troll Associates)
The Ayyam-i Ha Camel. Cher Holt-Fortin (Kalimat)
Camel. Caroline Arnold (Morrow Junior Books)
Camels. Jenny Markert (Child's World)
A Desert Year. Carol Lerner (Morrow Junior Books)
Deserts. Clint Twist (Macmillan)
Deserts. Lawrence Williams (Marshall Cavendish)
Deserts of the World. Jack Knowlton (HarperCollins)
Expanding Deserts. Paula Hogan (Gareth Stevens)
Exploring Deserts. Barbara Behm and Veronica Bonar (Gareth Stevens)
In the Desert. G. Stewart (Rourke)
Pamela Camel. Bill Peet (Holmes and Meier)
Twenty-Four Hours in a Desert. Barrie Watts (Watts)

VIDEOS

How the Camel Got His Hump. (Rabbit Ears Video)
The Living Planet: The Baking Deserts. (John D. and Catherine T. MacArthur Foundation Library Video Classics)
The Living Planet: The Margins of the Land. (John D. and Catherine T. MacArthur Foundation Library Video Classics)

PLACES TO VISIT

Metropolitan Toronto Zoo
Meadowvale Road
West Hill
Toronto, Ontario
M1E 4R5

San Diego Zoo
2920 Zoo Drive
San Diego, CA 92103

Auckland Zoological Park
Motions Road
Western Springs
Auckland 2
New Zealand

Brookfield Zoo
1st Ave. and 31st St.
Brookfield IL 60513

The Mugga Lane Zoo
RMB 5, Mugga Lane
Red Hill
Canberra, A.C.T. 2609
Australia

Granby Zoo
347 Bourget Street
Granby, Quebec
J2G 1E8

INDEX

Answers to CAMEL SECRETS questions:
1. b
2. c
3. c
4. b
5. b
6. a